DISCOVER

"THE ARMY GOES ROLLING ALONG"

A Tribute to the U.S. Army

Cherry Lake Press

Published in the United States of America by Cherry Lake Publishing
Ann Arbor, Michigan
www.cherrylakepublishing.com

Reading Adviser: Beth Walker Gambro, MS, Ed., Reading Consultant, Yorkville, IL

Photo Credits: Capt. Stephanie Snyder/DVIDS/Public Domain, cover, title page; SSG Antony Martinez/DVIDS/Public Domain, 5; American Unofficial Collection of World War I Photographs/National Archives, 7; Currier and Ives, CC0, via Wikimedia Commons, 8; Internet Archive Book Images, No restrictions, via Wikimedia Commons, 9; © STUDIO MELANGE/Shutterstock, 10; Department of Defense/Flickr, 11; SPC Marina Caggeso/DVIDS/Public Domain, 12; Shannon Collins/DVIDS/Public Domain, 13; Sgt. Alvin Conley/DVIDS/Public Domain, 14; SPC Kyara D Hutchinson/DVIDS/Public Domain, 15; CPO Lisa Ferdinando/DVIDS/Public Domain, 16; Rudolph D'Heureuse, who published a series of forty-one photos in 1863 ref Sorenson, Michael K. A Most Curious Corps. Military Images Magazine. Archived from the original on 2014-07-28. Retrieved on 13 February 2013. Public domain, via Wikimedia Commons, 17; Spc. Maribeth Kossman/DVIDS/Public Domain, 18; © The Old Major/Shutterstock, 19; Mark Olsen/DVIDS/Public Domain, 20

Cherry Lake Press is an imprint of Cherry Lake Publishing Group

Library of Congress Cataloging-in-Publication Data has been filed and is available at catalog.loc.gov.

Cherry Lake Publishing Group would like to acknowledge the work of the Partnership for 21st Century Learning, a Network of Battelle for Kids. Please visit Battelle for Kids online for more information.

Printed in the United States of America

TABLE OF CONTENTS

INTRODUCTION

U.S. Army Specialist Jessica Kwiatkowski wears her finest blue Army service uniform. The gold trim shines in the afternoon sun. She is from the 3rd U.S. Infantry Regiment of the Army, or "The Old Guard." It is the oldest U.S. Army **active duty** infantry unit. The soldier marches with measured steps. This is her last walk. Family, friends, and other soldiers are gathered. She hands off her rifle. She removes her gloves and sunglasses. She lays roses down for unknown soldiers.

This ends her service as a guard of the **Tomb** of the Unknown Soldier in Arlington National Cemetery. This sacred ground honors **unidentified** U.S. military members who died in combat. Army Tomb Guards protect the tomb 24 hours a day, 7 days a week. They have the honor and responsibility of keeping the memory of the lost alive.

The United States Army is older than the United States itself, formed as a colonial fighting force. Today, the U.S. Army has around 453,000 active duty members. They serve in over 200 different roles. They are ground forces, mechanics, accountants, surgeons, pilots, teachers, and many more.

Over the years, many have served. Many have died. All should be honored.

"THE U.S. ARMY" / "THE ARMY GOES ROLLING ALONG"

"The Army Goes Rolling Along" is the official song of the U.S. Army. The Army adopted the song in 1956. The music was written by Edmund L. Gruber in 1908. The current lyrics were written by Harold W. Arberg.

March along, sing our song,
with the Army of the free.
Count the brave, count the true,
who have fought to victory.

★ **ARMY FACTS** George Washington wasn't just the first president of the United States. Before that, he was the first commander in chief of the Continental (now U.S.) Army. Every member of the U.S. Congress voted for his selection.

We're the Army and proud of our name!
We're the Army and proudly proclaim:

LOOK

Look at this historical image of Army soldiers. How do they look different from modern soldiers you see in this book?

★ **ARMY FACTS** The name "Army" comes from the French language. *Armée* (ar-MAY) is French for "armed forces." *Armé*, without an extra *e* on the end, is French for "armed."

First to fight for the right,
And to build the Nation's might,
And the Army goes rolling along.

★ **ARMY FACTS** The Continental Army formed in June 1775. It protected 13 **colonies**. The Declaration of Independence was signed on July 4, 1776. After that, the Army fought for the new United States in the American Revolutionary War (1775–1783).

Proud of all we have done,
Fighting till the battle's won,
And the Army goes rolling along.

★ **ARMY FACTS** During the American Civil War (1861–1865), **immigrants** played a key role in the **Union** Army. They made up 25 percent of its troops! Many left jobs to fight for the Union.

Then it's hi! hi! hey!
The Army's on its way.
*Count off the **cadence** loud and strong;*

ASK QUESTIONS

What questions do you have about Army life in 1778? Write them down. Then ask a librarian, teacher, or other trusted adult to help you find answers.

★ **ARMY FACTS** An official **motto** of the U.S. Army is "This We'll Defend." It was first used in 1778. Army soldiers were working hard to defend the young United States against Britain. The Army continues to work to defend and preserve the United States today.

For where'er we go,
You will always know
That the Army goes rolling along.

★ **ARMY FACTS** While the Navy is known for the sea and the Air Force for the skies, the Army is known for the ground. In fact, elite Army paratroopers are known for diving out of planes to get back to the ground!

Valley Forge, Custer's ranks,
San Juan Hill and Patton's tanks,
And the Army went rolling along.

★ **ARMY FACTS** The U.S. Army has been using tanks since World War I (1914–1918). Tanks were built to break through enemy lines during **trench warfare**. Today, the Army uses the M1 **treads** Abrams battle tank. It has advanced weaponry, technology, and safety features.

Minute men, from the start,
Always fighting from the heart,
And the Army keeps rolling along

★ **ARMY FACTS** The Minutemen were elite **militia** soldiers in the 1600s and 1700s. They were always quick to get ready and the first to fight. People said they were "ready at a minute's notice."

Then it's hi! hi! hey!
The Army's on its way.
Count off the cadence loud and strong;

MAKE A GUESS

Why do you think discipline is important in the Army? How can it make the Army stronger? Make a guess!

"Discipline is the soul of an Army. It makes small numbers formidable; procures success to the weak, and esteem to all."
– George Washington, 1759

For where'er we go,
You will always know
That the Army goes rolling along.

★ **ARMY FACTS** The Army assists people in need during natural disasters. Army soldiers help with evacuation. They help with search and rescue and medical care. They help with safety and security. They help with housing.

Men in rags, men who froze,
Still that Army met its foes,
And the Army went rolling along.

★ **ARMY FACTS** Audie Murphy (1925–1971) was an Army soldier. He is the most decorated soldier in U.S. Army history. He served for 27 years and earned 19 individual awards. They include two Silver Stars for bravery in combat. He is buried in Arlington National Cemetery.

Faith in God, then we're right,
And we'll fight with all our might,
As the Army keeps rolling along.

★ **ARMY FACTS** There used to be a U.S. Army Camel Corps. In 1855, Congress gave money to the Army to buy camels from North Africa and the Middle East. But the camels were ill-suited for combat. The Camel Corps experiment ended with the start of the American Civil War.

Then it's hi! hi! hey!
The Army's on its way.
Count off the cadence loud and strong;
(two! three!)

THINK

Why do you think it's important to honor and respect Army soldiers who have served our country?

★ **ARMY FACTS** Millions of Americans are Army **veterans**. Of all U.S. military veterans, about 44 percent served in the Army. Those who served are Army soldiers for life, forever honored for their service.

For where'er we go,
You will always know

★ **ARMY FACTS** The Army has 76 active Army posts at home and abroad. The United States is home to 58 of them. Virginia and Texas have the most. There are nine Army posts in Virginia. There are five in Texas. There are also 18 overseas.

"The soldier is the Army. No army is better than its soldiers. The Soldier is also a citizen. In fact, the highest obligation and privilege of citizenship is that of bearing arms for one's country."

– General George S. Patton

That the Army goes rolling along!
(keep it rolling!)
And the Army goes rolling along!

CREATE

Work with family, friends, and neighbors to create a care package of American goods that overseas service members may miss from home. Choose an overseas U.S. Army base to mail the package to.

THE SOLDIER'S CREED

I am an American Soldier.
I am a warrior and a member of a team.
I serve the people of the United States, and live the Army Values.
I will always place the mission first.
I will never accept defeat.
I will never quit.
I will never leave a fallen comrade.
I am disciplined, physically and mentally tough, trained and proficient in my warrior tasks and drills.
I always maintain my arms, my equipment and myself.
I am an expert and I am a professional.
I stand ready to deploy, engage, and destroy, the enemies of the United States of America in close combat.
I am a guardian of freedom and the American way of life.
I am an American Soldier.

LEARN MORE

BOOKS

Banks, Anita. *US Army*. Mendota Heights, MN: North Star Editions, 2022.

Barrett, Mo. *Life in the U.S. Army*. North Mankato, MN: Capstone, 2024.

Leed, Percy. *The U.S. Army in Action*. Minneapolis, MN: Lerner Publications, 2023.

WEBSITES

Search these online sources with an adult.

The Army Goes Rolling Along with lyrics – The Army Song - Patriotic | Music & Lyrics | Video

United States Army Facts for Kids | Kiddle

GLOSSARY

active duty (AK-tiv DOO-tee) describing a member of the U.S. Armed Forces who works for the military full-time and can be deployed

cadence (KAY-duhns) the beat or count of a rhythmic pattern, as in marching

colonies (KAH-luh-neez) an area under the control of a foreign nation

immigrants (IH-muh-gruhnts) people who come to a country to live there permanently

militia (muh-LIH-shuh) group of citizens organized for military service

motto (MAH-toh) short expression or guiding principle

tomb (TOOM) structure built to hold the bodies of one or more dead people

treads (TREDZ) a system of connected metal plates that wrap around the wheels of a vehicle; spread out weight and increase grip

trench warfare (TRENCH WOR-fehr) battles that take place in long ditches dug in the ground

unidentified (uhn-iye-DEN-tuh-fied) not having a known identity

Union (YOON-yuhn) Northern states that fought and won against the Confederacy in the American Civil War

veterans (VEH-tuh-ruhnz) former members of the armed forces

INDEX